APPROACHING SABBATHS: POEMS

ALSO BY JENNIFER RAHIM

Poetry

Mothers Are Not the Only Linguists
Between the Fence and the Forest

Fiction

Songster and other Stories

ACKNOWLEDGEMENTS

"Lady Lazarus in the Sun", "Miss I-Tired", "For the Seeds that Wither", "The Wild Cat", "The Mango", "My Mother Took It", "Saint Francis and the Douen", first appeared in *New Caribbean Poetry: An Anthology* edited by Kei Miller, Carcanet Press, 2007. "My Mother Took It" was published in *Las Palabras Pueden: Los Escritores Y La Infancia*, UNICEF, Colombia, 2007. "The Mango" appeared in *Esta Riqueza Abandonada: Poesia Latinoamericana y Caribena*. Ed. Kundan Kanan. Trans. Shyama Prasad Ganguly and Meenakshi Sundriyal, Sahitya Akademi y Grulac, New Delhi, India, 2006.

APPROACHING SABBATHS: POEMS

JENNIFER RAHIM

P E E P A L   T R E E

First published in Great Britain in 2009
Peepal Tree Press Ltd
17 King's Avenue
Leeds LS6 1QS
UK

ISBN 13: 9781845231156

 Peepal Tree gratefully acknowledges Arts Council support

CONTENTS

POEMS RAIN

A RETURN TO QUINAM BAY

POSTSCRIPT

A SAINT FOR US

PORTRAIT I

Stamped there
    a kind of small animal fear
like some bird   caught off
its way   missed most.

A broad brow
often pleated   listening
it seems
to some distant sound
sensed
    more than heard.

The brown skin
        home to continents
no longer countable –
        still youthful
    but not untroubled.
Around the mouth
seriousness settles –
shield
to a great inner deep.

The lips
    kept pursed
as if holding back
    a flood of words.
    The white background
reaches in
so that she hovers
between worlds
and it is to another place
her gaze travels
        to the one
with whom her anguish conversed.

A BRIEF CONVERSATION

He: "My first childhood memory is about death."

She: "How old were you?"

He: "I think I was three, maybe four. I remember
sitting on the neighbour's step as the funeral procession filed past,
my hands tightly folded
across my chest."

She: "Why? What was wrong with your hands?"

He: "You mean you don't know that one?
About pointing at the dead?"

She shook her head.

He: "Your fingers will rot and fall off."

She: "No. I never heard that before."

He: "Well, it's been an obsession with me —
trying to track down my first memory.
But I think that's the one."

She: "Funny, how you remembered death.
It never occurred to me — pinpointing
my earliest memory. That's a hard one.
So many things have passed."

They parted then and she wondered why,
at that juncture, she had lied.

OPENING UP

She believed he understood suffering –
and he did. Really.

Yet, cautiously, she prefaced by saying,
"I have never told a man my story."

He nodded respectfully
and waited.

So she opened up
and tried to explain her sadness.

He listened. Really.
She waited.

At length he said,
"So that means you're not interested in sex."

They both burst out laughing
and remained friends.

Really.

FIRST COMMUNION DAY

On First Communion Day she felt a fraud
dressed all in white like a bride.

Her sins chimed like nursery rhymes
in the confessional – all sang in perfect time,

but one. No metre could order its horror.
She prayed the others would cancel it out.

But, after kneeling beneath the crucifix,
she still felt dirty by her fix.

"Why so sad?" her mother asked.

"I don't like my dress."

"But you look beautiful. So innocent."

"What will the boys wear?"

"Black trousers and white shirts," she said.

"How come they get to wear black?"

"Well, I suppose boys are allowed a little dirt,"
she said, laughing.

"Then you should dress me like them."

BLACK POWER APRIL, 1970

In April she turned seven.
The city was an army of arms, uplifted —
fists, tight, punching hard at heaven.

What did it all mean — becoming seven,
and Port-of-Spain an angry sea,
heaving, demanding release?

Sister preached a mad Sermon on Hair,
led blind prayers to the Virgin for peace —
her lenses as black as her fear.

Corralled in a rosary of responses,
she saw again the white of her father's shirt,
sailing to work. More than anything,

she wanted to march beside him, cuffing
against the wrong she could not tell him,
shouting, "Power!" until the whole sky fell.

THOSE AUGUST DRUMS, UNCLE

He wanted to be a musician. Yet,
no one danced or sang through his sessions.
There was no conversation.

He played electric guitar and drums.
She remembered mostly his driving,
frenzied beat pitched beyond recognition –

pounding even while the house slept.
In August, her body rocked like a ship
on a high and troubled sea.

A black man in the seventies beating
to Kiss, Iron Maiden and Led Zeppelin LPs
should have raised an alarm.

They listened, pinned down, stunned
by the sound. Someone should have known
something was very wrong.

WASHING DISHES WITH A CRAB IN THE SINK

A stool brought her waist-high with the sink,
right for dishwashing chores on market day
when the bound crab lay among the dishes.

It wasn't easy staying focused on soiled cups
and plates with those cautious, pop-up eyes
becoming every passing minute warring clubs —

for the creature issued a firm challenge
on her unbounded life, while flat on its back,
drowning in soapsuds, gundies strapped

with vine, their power harnessed but alive,
down to the twitching claws of the legs
that practised running though tied.

Dishwashing with the crab in the sink
held a lesson she needed most to master:
how to fight free from being held under.

EULOGY FOR AKIEL

Akiel, they found you kneeling
at the bottom of a water chamber,

holy Mecca on your mind
as the darkness broke into you,

big-boy heat spinning cobwebs
inside your innocence.

I hear the drums of conscience
pounding down the doors of Guinea,

insisting: look into your grave –
mirror of our betrayal.

What words could you pray
against reason eclipsed by so great

an evil, it stole your very name? The sin
is ours, Akiel. It is our turn to kneel,

beg forgiveness that not mighty Allah,
Christ – not even Anansi could spin a trick

to set you free. There is no comfort
in blaming gods for omissions to see

the gilded web begin its sly purpose,
so bewitched by a spell that whips

us still, makes us smiling Toms
still, the forbidding tongue silenced,

willing to let you slip through the cracks
to save the false gods we venerate.

I hear the Atlantic opening her tombs
and dry bones planning revolution.

Akiel, no God will deny you company.
We must pray for mercy.

A GROWING DARK
(for Sean Luke)

Dogs sniffed him out
already becoming dust
in a shallow grave

a stone's throw away
from the house where love
anointed him an angel.

I imagine: someone stood
bewildered on a mound,
raw as though tilled

for a fresh planting
where no more harvests came,
but saw nothing, heard

without understanding
the leaves' complaint, smelt,
faintly, the last burning,

while his blood raged
a pitch too high and the stalk
rooted in his bowels

made vinegar every grain
of sugar. In the end,
the dogs trailed

the death stench –
much too late for Sean
and Amy and Akiel – all lost

right beneath our noses.
So it was relief to find him,
wear black, blink headlights

in broad daylight, bark
demands to see the faces
of criminals – mere children,

but twisted like neglected
fields of cane. There is cheap
comfort in laying blame –

now, when the mouths
of babes, too, are blind
and scarce truth falls

flat to ground
where even angels stumble
in a growing dark.

SHE DREAMS OF FALLING

She dreams of falling from a great height –
over and over again,
her body a bridge
someone exploded – and the chorus singing
falling down,
falling down (my fair
lady) on and on . . .

she descends through unending space –
pieces of her at a time – arms, legs, breasts,
her entire head coming apart,
fragments of her self
small, fragile parts
falling down. . .
but never hitting ground . . . and the children
waiting to collapse
laughing
before they rise to start again

when her eyes catch sight of her hips
passing by
on the way down
she wants to ask *Is it really that easy. . .*
falling? But she can't find her mouth
and the bridge is holding *whole way up*,
swaying, waiting to hit the ground
only she doesn't want to –
doesn't want the shadows on top of her,
hands all over her, getting soiled,
especially down there
(*my fair*
lady)
not being a good girl any more
good for nothing any more

                    the rough voice on and on
in her head warning
not to tell
and everything is falling
down
        and
                down

until
a faceless woman
begins catching all her parts
in the net she has made of her skirt
and when every one is cradled in folds
that look like clouds,
she puts her back together again
where she lies on the bed

so the dream can never end. . .

LETTING THE PIECES FALL

A remarkable peace is here. Is it you?
Now that I am standing on a black rock,
facing a heady ocean, thinking what freedom
to fear nothing, words come rushing back
to me like waves hurl themselves at the shore,
expecting embrace. *The noise here is itself –*
a fullness overflowing to sound past hearing.
Is it you or me speaking… My peace?

Many things come to me in dreams,
not because I am becoming my mother,
her womb bleeding prophecy.

I dream to escape a woman
who is perpetually tidying up after me, meticulous
as shame. I dream another explodes a wave

lets the pieces fall.

THERE WILL BE TIME ENOUGH FOR LAUGHTER

There will be time enough for laughter
when this long night is over
and daylight is forever.

There will be time to be the child
you never were, when play is for fields,
not always concealed.

Believe me: there will come a time
your screams will be pure pleasure
and comfort flowing over.

There will be rest with magical dreams,
not terror, and you will walk,
as you imagined, on sunbeams.

Yes, I believe there will come a time
for rejoicing, for you with the sad eyes
and tongue always tied.

There is a day you will stand next
to a stranger and point out yourself
circa nineteen whatever and say,

"I wasn't bright, but I was so happy
as a child." And both will smile
and shout, "Yippy!"

Believe me: Akiel, Sean, Amy
(of names too many), there are those
who survive and remember only

to learn to speak,
no matter how imperfectly,
of your dream and theirs

to be first mere children.
For now, we, the unbright, mourn
for the dawn of right.

THE SECRET OF FRUIT BEARING TREES
(for Malcolm)

Is a secret my daddy teach me, he said,
sounding like a boy of ten.
I saw him back then swallowed up
in his daddy's tall tops, sitting
flat on the ground,
belly full, committing
saplings to fertile holes.

They bear fast that way – fruit big so
weigh the branches down.
My daddy teach me. The repeat,
lingered, quivering in the shade
of something unnamed.

We both looked at his hands:
continents of strength, empty –
promises of plenty. He laughed
and tucked them away – that day.

I had only half believed his tale.

So when the story came, too late,
of the axe that chased his bride
until her heart withered and died
from the terror he had planted there,
I went out among the trees and sang
lullabies to each trembling leaf.

Now I reap sweetness every season,
still half-believing, still wondering
what was her harvest he so feared
he could not bear.

LADY LAZARUS IN THE SUN

It must always be done
this business of rising from the grave
like some stubborn sun

I practise on instruction
     Just do it
put my shoes on, take up
the weight a body gathers
and walk across dark waters

No real miracle
for those whose faith could fly
even with irons for sandals
walk the Atlantic light

But I have to manage it —
with my skin
watered down to brightness
as a salvation

My feet, a history,
heavy with El Dorado gold,
brown sugar madness
ole' time sailor sweetness

Watch how I step into the ring
showing my motion
my body a beauty,
a prize,
prised too early
for a taste of sugar
dumplin,
sugar
cake

down the middle
passage
way
from darkness

Smile please lady
forget the bitter taste of cane

II

at least once a month
this coming back from the slips –
bleeding the agony of blank
the broken plank
the free fall –
O lord, my brain, my brain
howls an unspeakable knowledge
of unremembered things
I try to learn its language
This blackout, a saviour –
dark mother when you poke
prod, probe me –
the blank you read in me
the giddy decline to nothing
the going under I feel
is your judgement text

Read between the blank
for stealing my sex

III

Another month and
I have come back again
and you are pleased thinking
soon she will be breakfast-toast-

brown again
ready for jam again,
milk in your coffee again
currency
playing the fool on TV
selling island sun
Vat 19 rum
with natural coppertone
mildly processed curls-
preferred girl
And I will be, as you want me,
grateful for my fix
callaloo theory,
carnival baby, global
everybody
        just easy

IV

But listen
I have lived with the dead
seven times seventy years
rotten anxiety shrouds me
bones rattle in my body
a girl sucking her thumb
still moans in me

Here
put your fingers where they
have pierced –
it *is* really me
don't be afraid
now you've had your piece

I come into the light
my skin paled in this grave
of rank usage
No, I will not be dancing
this time
to tunes that play me
for dead
        skin fried crisp as KFC
or shaking my sugar bumsey
because I have done it again
heard the call,
seen the light and said

Alleluia

said

Yes

picked up my bed, Amen
and kept on walking

V

I do this rising business
like I wash my body
sun my history
air my wounds
take off my death again
my dress again
stand the fierce heat of visibility
without sun-block
without mushroom umbrella
without Ray-Ban
stare straight the face

of golden brightness
becoming my Kali self
slowly
learning to take back my sun again
becoming the dark past brown
the woman no longer held under

I will love my darkness well

FOR WOMEN LIKE US

There must be a saint for women like us –
those who were never virgins,
never knew what grace is innocence.
I searched everywhere to find her,
rolled decades of beads to be near
the woman who could hold
all my sorrows in her lap,
halt this breakneck flight from myself.
And I have grown so strong
with flying people are amazed,
think me a wonder that speeds the skies,
not knowing how I hunger for rest
from the night that gave me wings,
made my tenderness an invincible core,
a strange thing – almost possible.
I have offered novenas on my knees,
bargained with heaven to be once
the woman denied me, the womb
where that power comes to ground.

There must be a saint for women like us –
those who will never woo a unicorn.

FOR SEEDS THAT WITHER

This is a beg pardon
for the seeds that wither
and get choked out before they flower

those fragile ones eager to bear
that rock-heart and shallow-mind
kill dead long before their time

For the unborn and all things just
beginning that meet sudden dry season
today I beg pardon

For all seeds that start to grow
in look-at-my-crosses spots of bird-drop
like concrete crack and old chamber pot

For the pawpaw plant that claim a space
right in Miss Mary rose-garden
and get root out for being too brazen

This is a prayer for all the little ones
that sex bandit rob of their innocence
Today I beg pardon

This is a chant to break the back
of the jumbie who busy building
fences to keep lines clearly drawn

like Amado Diallo who eat police bullet
for holding up a wallet in a pasture
he dreamt might to be greener

For all those we slam the life door on
who pass by without being mourned
today I beg pardon

This is a prayer for the down-and-out
the coke-heads and gone-crazy
the ones whose courage-tank run empty

This is a hymn for women like Bajan Patsy
that life and men beat up on
till body and soul-case split like a pod

This is a prayer that at least someone
will mourn and temples of rebirth rise
where their limbs meet with earth

Today I beg pardon
for seeds that wither and die
before they get a chance at life

APPROACHING SABBATHS

MISS I-TIRED

I hear her calling to the houses she knows.
At Lydia's gate, always stopping for a chat
and rest before she takes up her weight again,
holding the same pain at her waist, her head
leading her feet onward to the next station.
Dotsy's name sings out. A brief exchange.
Then she teases Nathaniel, coaxes him to speak.
He plays her game and pronounces a string
of indecipherable words. Her joy erupts,
embracing the entire mountain. Complete.
She moves on. Behind her, the entire ocean
straddles her back – all the time going up
to a home way past my seeing. Her eternal
prayer showering Rose Hill – *Lord, I so tired!*

MY MOTHER TOOK IT
(Grenada, August 2003)

My mother took it. Aaron standing with me
before Annadale Falls. A miracle shot really:
an August evening after rain, the light fading,
and Mummy awkward with the camera, shifting
this way and that, and we restrained by smiles
forgot to say *Flash!* She wouldn't take another.
For all my pleading simply said, *It'll be fine*.
With that being that, we climbed single file
like pilgrims leaving a shrine. Now, there it is,
with me wherever I go, the way we carry love:
Aaron leaning gently on my side, behind us
a pierced dark gushing water anoints his head,
and both of us beaming out at the woman
fumbling with the camera whose light was on.

MY MOTHER SANG

My mother sang no lullabies to soothe
us when we cried. I cannot remember
her songs, only her hands: tough palms
and chipped nails that dreamed to be long.
No. My mother never sang – not then
when her mothering was a pilgrimage
of doing whatever she could. She held
us strong with small hands that even now
seem strangers to tenderness, shy to give
what her endless labour never named, love.
I never knew her songs, but her stations
were a full-measure giving – the music
my heart secreted and now sings back to me
in the sweet tenor of my mother's voice.

AFTER THE FIRST SHOWER
(April 25th, 2006)

You wonder at the green so soon refreshed,
so grateful for brief relief, and the garden
still – this morning expectant, and glowing
as ginger lilies hold high brilliant torches
and bougainvillaeas spill rainbows over walls.
The grass – bleached or bare, elsewhere
wholly green – waits the dry season out.
You think that is what it's all about. The More –.
On this Feast of St. Mark the Evangelist,
the earth publishes her good news as plainly
as that scribe's hand, certain as the çicada's
fierce cry quickens the halls of the hospital
that wards my father, with no more voice
than his ripe thirst for the rain's full return.

SECOND SUNDAY AFTER EASTER

Down a long tunnel, doors closed on the left;
on the right, windows display bodies supine
or rolled on their sides, beyond – sunshine.
I remember the sign written blue on white,
taped like an afterthought at the entrance.
CAURA WARD –. Ceiling fans hummed,
circulating air the way that word became a fate.
Mother walks straightbacked to meet him,
with Aaron and I in her wake, hanging back.
Then we see him in a bed that margins
the hallway, breathing loudly from the neck.
We gather several paces away, hung
until Aaron calls *Granddad* – runs ahead.

GETTING THERE

Getting there, she joked about the day
he raved, *You are contradicting me,*
(on some matter she couldn't remember) –
he holding her gaze before storming out
to regain his calm among the plants,
puttering until darkness covered him
and she, turning on lights, called him in.
He came quietly, taking his own time,
and sat half-repentant in his chair.
I wondered – as we parked where yellow poui
cloaked naked earth – if the hurt she felt
equalled the defiance he held to save himself –
in the end, both of them, half, letting go.

THE GOING, UP

Take care you trip, I say. She laughs
in her girlish way, takes hold of the rail,
readying herself for the going, up.
It is our little joke – the way her life
has been a story of falls, unexpected
trip-ups that took her to ground.
I stand behind and watch her negotiate
her climb, one step at a time, ascending
the levels to where my father lies, flat out
on a line between not wanting the parting
and the sleep that means first letting go.
I watch that left ankle betray her ascent.
She chuckles, rights herself, and rises again.
Like these feet not for walking, she says.

DECIPHERING HIS MEANINGS

He has taken to writing – urgent letters
in upper case make words he cannot say.
Amazing the passion in his pen pressed
firmly on the white squares we bring him.
We read and he sits suspended in the gap
his words create between him and his writing,
waiting for us to catch up, meet him there,
in the centre of his pain. We're delayed
deciphering his meanings, holding out
the page as if longsighted and looking
at him on the bed's edge, a stranger – almost
much too distant to reach, and he puzzled
that being so near had become too far
for us to read his plain hand, precisely.

I TOUCH MY FATHER'S FEET

After the sporadic litany of asking,
the removal of what is no longer clean;
after ordering the untidiness of illness,
the storing things that anticipate need —
want being the one pain we played gods
strong enough to free him from. Dumb,
he looks through our chaos of caring,
and when there was nothing left to give,
my mother pops a ginger mint, inhales
deeply and casually surveys his body.
Then, as if taste releases fresh vision
asks me, gently, to rub my father's feet.
Now, my hands are her meditation,
and she, the face he gazes on —

AFTER HOSPITAL VISITS

She comes in like a wilted flower – spent,
slightly limping on a wounded ankle
that each year seemed less able to carry
her small frame on her heart's ready business.
Missions my father baptised her goings
to care for grandchildren – days at a time.
Something like pain trembled in his voice.
He needed her much more than he could say,
but bore her absences, as he did his suffering,
bravely – waiting as she once did for him
when his many goings were not about love.
Now, she is the woman of his sixth station.
After hospital visits she collapses in his chair
puts her feet up, and is no more broken –
bridge that bears his not too late love of home.

MOTHER LAUGHING, LAST

It is near eleven and the living-room
is suddenly silent, no longer groans low
with insistent television talk –
at last, switched off.

Small slippers raise a tired applause
with the tiles as she moves to pull
windows shut and blinds rattle down
to close with the usual struggle.

At the bathroom vanity she begins
her teeth-brushing session. Brisk strokes,
firm gargles before going in –
the bedroom already snoring.

Only this time her rhythm alters:
halts and staggers along as if drunk.
Sure scrubs: a pause, holding steady:
another brush: laughter peals out.

Something in her joy that night
I could not interrupt with any asking
what thought or memory so entertained her,
suddenly becoming light for her.

I was content to listen, marvelling.
And that is how I will remember her –
laughing last to make for easy going.

DADDY IN THE GARDEN

You must take the dead stuff off, he said.
And I watched him from the window,
sitting with the fern basket
like a patchy head between his legs.

They grow right when you trim them.
The second time to reassure himself
before his arms started working, slowly,
cutting, extracting anything
that was no longer green.

And I saw him again.
I was ten and between his knees,
after Saturday hairwashing,
in the sun spot between the guava
and mango trees, rough-drying my strands,
tugging me free of knots.

        Now he is an old man taking sun,
his grey straining light so his head shone
as he worked on where he was,
gently cutting away unwanted things.
I wondered if he knew
how I watched him
even today in the garden,
ordering the fern without hurry.

I found myself thinking
how much like a monk he looks
bent over the basket, perusing the leaves
like some sacred text,
        just happy being there.

LATE BLOOMER

My father was never a building man –
crude patcher of things,
until late gardens sprouted from his hands.

NEW STARTING POINT

This is my 70x7 entry – notes I jot down
about you. No, not the poem, just the steps
I make towards writing you. Lefty scribbles
that totter with outstretched arms, balancing,
holding the line – my way to meet your distance,
almost getting to where you stand like a stop.
Then and now, Daddy, you slip off my page.
My first syllable, the last hanging on the edge,
the rest dangling over unfathomable space.
Maybe to read you I have to go right over,
not make your everlasting word my anchor.
Even then, you will be, to me, unreadable –
right to left. Only this time, I will at last be
first, right on the left of a new starting point.

A SABBATH REMEMBERED

Grandma Coleen put shiny quarters
in our hands for Father's collection.

Every Sunday, during August holidays,
she packed us off to Mass,

as many as twelve, in scrambled-up
church clothes: sun-dried dresses

and trousers in flood, sleep hanging on,
as if churchgoing were an eviction.

We woke to the storm of her fussing
to get us ready and going, puzzled

by her zeal to keep faith with a doctrine
that seemed, then, only for children.

She never came; but our protests died
when those coins touched our palms

as we filed by. Bright quarters and
the solemnity of her giving were Mass

on Sunday. Not hours stuck in pews
exchanging whispered nonsense,

giggling at the psalmist who couldn't sing,
inventing words for every hymn, waiting

for when collection time came
and we were suddenly changed, sitting

meekly in our benches, if not asleep,
eyes anchored on our feet

as the basket sniffed the line, holding on
to our silver to the end when we wore

her face among the believers, going out,
chipping to tambourine and strings.

I know now churchgoing was a pact
we made with her to feed our hunger

for the temptations in Mr. Fred's parlour:
milk biscuits sweeter than Father's wafer,

heavy yellow cakes, wicked preserves
we ate in haste like Sabbath Hebrews

to spare ourselves the licks we imagined,
but never came. She never asked

where the money went as we passed
into her fold, with the sea playing

behind her back, her swimsuit swinging
the line – her face alive as the surf.

SEAWALL

Back of stone and ugly concrete
kept at bay
the encroaching sea.

We loved and resented it:
heard its throaty sighs
when the tide,

inch by inch,
delivered the deep, stroked
alive its barnacled side.

The wall bore its station
honestly. Give it that.
Caught between worlds

with no claim on any,
steupsed or gargled idly.
Spoke no words

but made ballads
of its woes. Not like us
who feigned content

to better our chances
of getting in —
not shouting or fighting,

spent hours nailed
to a backdoor-Calvary
where she would appear

drying her hands
in her apron, ignoring
our vigil to stare

like an indifferent Pilate
at the horizon
while we suffered our fate.

The sea —
we never got enough of it,
were land-sentenced Atlantians

nursing loss
until one nod freed us,
wild exiles scampering

to reclaim our country.
The seawall
was our tarmac down.

First, the short sprint,
angling left
before, sprung to space,

feet fast-pedalling air
as though bereft of earth
too late, wanting

the upward turn,
not the plunge to deeper birth.
It was like falling

to ground
in a turgid lung,
then scuttling up

liquid rungs to explode,
as after a baptism.
We repeated returns,

crossing terrains
while the wall stood firm –
thinking nothing

of its vocation –
bridge over
both sides of heaven.

FISHING

Spending August
by the sea, we learned

to fish early: how to bait
a hook for a bite,

cast far your silver
without wounding the fisher.

How to read the tension
on a finger,

work a line to tease the deep,
or time the yank

that provokes the leap,
when your fish, too philosophical

to eat, suddenly weighs loss
greater than lasting sleep.

As many as twelve
learned the art, but not all

fished well, not having
the same passion for waiting,

not the hauling in
that hooks the heart.

SYBIL

I remember her stationed at the Singer,
the mountain window framing her
leaning in, without strain, to spotlight
as she tended the fabric's flight.

Sylvan fingers, made it seemed
for different labour, like the kneading
that coaxes soil to yield, guided
fine garments into being,

extracted pins with precision timing
before the needle landed and bit in.
Mystery upflowed from under the table
where her feet, wed to pedal,

beat a wing that drove her purpose
as from another world to surface
where she worked stitched to form
in undying dawn.

Her language was a garbled chug
fast-gathering to zing in uneven metre,
not erratic, but like a rhythm
to which she was medium.

I understood nothing,
but the days spent collecting
the leftovers of her trade — pins, thread,
material ends — were to me bread

now rising in me like prophecy's yeast.

MATINS

A candle held beside an open Bible
made her small kitchen a chapel.
Shadows grew alert and tall, ascended
walls to veil her head as she read
like a seasoned nun praying matins.
The low drone of her psalms ebbed more
than flowed from that vault. Axiomatic:
a simple wisdom. In the soft light
preceding dawn her breath washed the house
in easy measure – hushed as the heartbeat
of her flame. It was her hour to peer
at use-wrinkled pages – suppliant.
She churned familiar words. Was all ear,
as one sensing the ocean's nearing.

UNCLE KENNETH

Sunday morning was hot bakes and cheese,
chocolate tea flavoured with nutmeg and spice.

Much too full for play, waiting on lunch
was watching Grandma Sybil turn her pots.

For hours, with Jim Reeves singing hymns
on the neighbour's stereo and she humming,

her kitchen was haloed with seasoned incense
as chicken stewed, crab and callaloo cooked,

rice boiled and macaroni pies baked to gold.
We did small chores while she officiated

at the stove, glancing up every now and
then to scan the road, watching, we knew,

for her one Sabbath prophecy to materialise:
Uncle Kenneth, arriving exactly on time

armed with a bundle of fresh watercress
and his smile constant as his ungreying head.

Belly-pleasing dishes and Uncle Kenneth's
bitter greens made her Sunday meal complete.

CHATHAM

I

Chatham: village whose name thrusts
and drums off breath and tongue
as the double pulse of a fired piston,
or heartbeat driving relentlessly on
without ambiguity about its mission.

In these days of dread losses
and crude plenty, the nation's anthem
is a song piped through petrol pumps,
chorused by gross industry of all kinds.
Chatham, small mouth crying up

from deep country,
is the conscience of this cataract-I-
sland, chipping dim-sighted
down the road to a wilderness
masquerading as a promised land.

Shut-up and we are sold to a future
already diseased by lies traded
as assurances, sick betrayals to safe-
guard toxic windfalls. So speak on.
Gather us into a multitude, one shout

that will bring Jericho down,
in this time, lest we become exiles
on the soil that roots and holds us –
will love us but not spare our errors.

Chatham: Chatham: Chatham:

II

Listen, something quickens here,
pristine as what matters always is,
will call us back to ourselves

as mothers do on evenings,
calling play-wild children in
to a simple house pregnant

with the scents of love,
ordinary as the glow of a stove
pulses low as a hand stirs.

Something is here, alive as breath
always reminds us of ourselves
while we labour and build,

growing too large for the castle
of ourselves, forgetful of ourselves,
it approaches as a pirogue

laden with the ocean targets
the distant shore, the anchorage
that completes every voyage.

Something eternal turns in worlds
fishermen net on a beach where sea
washes us without bias or cost,

nourishing beyond measure.
This peninsula is enough treasure.
Trees still speak an ancient tongue,

chant mantras, hymns, prayers
even the deaf will hear – clear
as a sky of winged green screams

its passage over. Earth weds us one.
Now is the time for love
strong as a jealous God's.

Something moves like prophecy
in rivers this land secrets
in its belly – pure

as the language poets search for
and priests long to preach.
Chatham: Filter us for a future

where water, wind, earth and air
neighbour us as skin vests heart
and soul for a seamless dawn.

Chatham: Chatham: Chatham:
heartland: mantra: beat on.

GRANDE RIVIERE'S BEAUTY

Grande Riviere's beauty is the other side
of its pain. This is also my truth to face,
but being so near I had to come this far
to find it. No longer a fishing village,
now a stop for tourists and weekend naturalists,
you sense the invasion the villagers feel
in their obsession with signs prohibiting, *by law,*
a host of offences – trespassing, hunting,
littering, parking, standing, turning...
Stay long enough in any place and its suffering
will lay aside the masks you put on its face
when you first came. Stay long enough,
and the shadows that neighbour your radiance
will surface to join company with the life
taking breeze at the street corners.

TURTLE-WATCH GRANDE RIVIERE

Hundreds of them
tiny flippers churning
in basins that withhold the ocean.
That's how we keep them safe.
Then   pointing to the sky   *corbeaux*
and after a pause   *dogs*.   He picks up one
holds it in his palm like a reluctant asterisk.
I ask who owns the dogs. *Villagers*
he says *they don't want to tie them.*
We both watch the hatchlings   frantic
in their dry cells,   every limb
straining,   moving like thread mills.
I cannot feel grateful.

We let them go at six. More make it that way.
It is twenty after three.
The hours seem an eternity   too long
to taste the ocean's salt.   *Watch this*
he says and places one on the sand
its head facing the almond trees.   *See,*
they always know which way to go. Pleased
he retrieves the leatherback   the limbs
working like an automated car. I ask
How do they find the sea? He shrugs
puts it back in *They just know what they know*
I think W*hat better reason to let them go*
and move to make my own turn *Wait*
he calls   *that will cost you ten*
You have to pay to see them.

THE ROAD THROUGH LA VEGA
(for R.A.)

The road through La Vega village appeared,
just as I took the stretch where the gradient
left of Rose Hill's corner becomes steeper,
and bamboo patches and trees make a canopy
pierced by soft light. This sudden marriage
of places, the way love or grief comes –
unexpectedly, a reminder of the powers
that disarm us, giving back the flesh we fear
to love, as we must the suffering in ourselves.
So you are here with me, on this northern strip
of our island, but driving us through its heart
to Tabaquite, along a route green with singing,
but too short for the things we almost said
that years later would be too late for us
to believe strong enough to cross the bridge
our being together, at that moment, built.

I HEARD IT

I heard it — just a strain as the car negotiated
the bridge, and the wheels raised a complaint
on steel plates that hushed the drunken
democracy of voices celebrating its bounty.
I felt it — the small pulse — tucked away
                        amid all that was singing.
It hung on the brink of every noise, holding
a taut distance like one gauging welcome.

There, on that rust-wounded bridge that wailed
as if my crossing caused pain, I stopped —
right in the middle of it, with Shark River
tripping under, the air a marketplace of chatter.
My listening held ground, long, but nothing —
the nearing was all sound....

TODO IS THE FEAST
(July 3rd)

Today is the feast day of St. Thomas,
the one who touched to heal his heart.
St. Thomas, the twin, split by his doubt
and knowing – the very thing, double-
faced and questioning that makes us
almost pity him, hold him in suspension,
not quite welcomed until: *My Lord
and my God!* The light switches on
and finally we can see him whole not split,
not needing to be intimate with wounds,
testing the limits to get at what is real.
I think his sainthood is his question,
not the response that lets us off the hook –
saves us from what we fear to know.

THE WILD CAT
(July 22nd)

The wild cat was prowling again last night.
I heard her padded paws pacing the porch.
I didn't leave the light on. That must have attracted her –
she likes playing in the dark. It is her time
to put on her amber torches to search me out.
The truth is we have been looking for each other,
only I am reluctant to let her in the house.
I think of the ruction and scandal she will cause.
Mostly, I fear she will devour me;
but she is growing impatient. Some mornings
I see her prints on my door and once
she left a dead thing on the chair
where I sit to watch the ocean lap the shore.
But change is in the air. To my surprise,
I left my key in the door last night.

CATCHING THE RAYS
(August 6th)

I have decided to get as much sun as possible,
take my chances with the UV rays, give up
living in the shade like the lily I could never be.
I have refused again the café au lait story, stopped
wearing sunglasses to tone down the brightness.
Better to risk blindness than settle for only
half-seeing the shining. Light makes the insides
unafraid to befriend the unnamed – the leaves,
they know it. They feed their roots this faith:
to trust deeper their underground growing.
I have decided to remove the veil, sit in my yard
taking sun like Terry, the day before she died,
blackening to the rocks of Gouyave, changed
to the colour of light when you see it, head on.

SAINT FRANCIS AND THE DOUEN

(after reading Galway Kinnell)

The head
sheltered by a great mushroom hat
holds the secret of all things beginning
and the wisdom of their endings.
Hidden there
is the knowledge of mysteries unbaptised,
tiny, faceless creatures –
those knots of possibility are the dread
beneath the hat.
Hidden there
is a mouth crying in the forests,
calling the living to step
beyond the boundary of their seeing;

but sometimes it is necessary
to reach out and cradle the child,
and tell again in touch and sweet lullaby
of its loveliness and wonderful promise;
as Saint Francis did
when he followed the small voice
that beckoned him from the darkness,
then stooped low to where the infant sat
naked on a wet riverbank,
swaddled in the mud of all things beginning;
and reaching to take the child into his arms
he saw his face look back at him,
right there, from the water's surface,
and in that moment's recognition
found again the gift of self-blessing –
for all things rise to life again, from within,
in the waters of self-blessing;
so the Saint gently removed the hat
in a sun-bathed spot witnessed by the river,

the earth, the trees and the passing breeze,
and with healing touch and soft song
sang of the infant's perfect loveliness;
from the tender head and troubled brow,
the shy, half-formed face
and the small wounded heart,
he blessed the whole length of the body;
from the upstretched arms
to the strange, backward turn of the feet,
he blessed their high intelligence
to brave the abandoned places
only to save what was theirs alone to give,
blessed again and again that perfect beauty
until the child became sunlight,
forever shining within —
of self-blessing.

POEMS RAIN

ORACLE

Is it you: spirit that strikes
a room dumb: shadow
slipping by the lazy eye?

They look but pretend
to be found: nailing truth
and toasting salvation.

Never where they gather,
still you salt their talk:
nourish their gossip to myth.

Prescient footfall, drum-
call, sounding what they
fear and most want to hear.

They come, tripping up
your mountain like weekend
pilgrims you-whoing

an approach that doubles
back to question them
that call you out:

babbling tongue of leaves
scripting breeze,
ears pinned to ground,

mining for rhythms up-
sprung as a wren's song,
or water filtering down.

POETRY

That morning a far blue
tugged the eye

like a line anchored to a kite
that soared

just beyond vision
and looking was an up-

ward reach as a child
beholds the world on

tiptoe – wanting more.
It is the height past

the burden of signs
that wings the heart.

Or else seeing
is the marlin's way –

full-bellied with strain
between earth and sky

as if starved of both
or approaching a birth.

JOHN

It begins a slight tremor
like the twang of a plucked string –
a sonorous, elastic wail lodged
between heartbeat and gut-feel.

Waves wed to a single line –
stretched through time. The note held
to fullness is a border. Its calling long –
if there is such a measure

for the date and hour a language
takes possession of your tongue.

But you know it – as from the womb
a child hears a great beauty channel
a prayer pitched to a seat so high,
it seduces and escapes the ear,

slips by an ordinary rhyme like a God leaps
joyously to greet what explodes the line
or raging blind enters vision
where a desert makes you citizen:

mouth seasoned on a simple creed:
locusts to clear paths: wild honey
to release wisdom-speak.

ELIZABETH

She lives in us all,
the unbearing we carry
to full term, flesh

of our flesh, growing
to its end – even what is barren
ripens to completion.

Look, the mule conceives
a prophet: a pregnant mouth
converts the breeze.

There: the one thing missing
hangs ready
on the greening tree,

arched as a bow, or domed
as a woman's belly –
stretched to release.

But first, the long labour:
grieving womb or dry unrising
delivers the promise.

A VERSION OF ZECHARIAH'S SPELL

I shall speak only after you —
until then I hold your sayings in my hand
like a shell, some crustacean's house
discarded, but colour-lush, still, perfect.

Perfection not being your truth,
I shall say nothing, but tenant your meaning:
my hand cupped like one sensing
not knowing the treasure held.

So I make the round of every town,
like a mendicant with no good news flowing
from my tongue, only a beggar's palm,
half-extended, with no real need for alms.

I shall speak only when you swell in me
like a wave full and ready — cresting,
terror, and peace when unfurled, finally,
like the frill that borders this shell.

For now, I am the silent one — . Struck dumb,
I carry you around, — with no story to tell
until the underside of me flips up,
breaks your spell, and I, the one held.

POEMS RAIN

Some poems never get written, never bless
a page as rain pours down its blessings
just for the sake of giving, like when it came
as I walked one evening and a man called to me
from his house, *Yeh, taking Jah blessing?*
I smiled because he was so absolutely right.
Poems have been raining on me for years,
but I keep running for shelter under eaves,
hugging myself under trees, dodging the drips,
intent on keeping myself dry. It seems
I have been walking under umbrellas all my life,
afraid to throw back my face and let heaven
wash me, and be well pleased.

THE MANGO

I am told the great Buddha found rest
in the shade of a mango tree,

that the fruit is food of the gods
and the blossoms Cupid's love arrows

or Manmatha's darts. Or else the mango
is the wish-granting tree, and its juice

cleanses the body of impurities.
For Goodison its sweetness is poetry.

I wish I'd known these stories
when I was a girl among its branches

begging freedom from an ugly love,
eating so I may never touch the ground.

Perhaps this knowing is right on time
like Saraswati's gift of learning,

for now I know my hard passage
to be blessed since my child's prayer

rose in the fragrance of heaven,
and today poems flow in my blood

becoming sunlight with each season
as the ambrosial flesh of mangoes.

ON REACHING THE AGE PAST EXPLAINING

and so you ask me
what have I been doing
now that the shelf is my home –
speaking all the time
to the face on my breasts
I suppose you see –

and to my surprise
I discover the breeze
always blows gently
off the land at evening
and the sea is cool
as age past explaining

and so what if my skirt
swells like a ready wave
and the hips you swore
were made for children
reveal only words
resting in a dark cradle

and so what if the thunder
of my arrival on the pages
of these islands
makes feet run backwards
what if the sand mutes my voice

to a softened sizzle
look,
my hands lift with the palms
and sway like a shouter
in spirit,
and in my armpits
words gather like coconuts

full of life-giving water —
so what if you ask

what if I have nothing
but a head nutty with verse,
at evening, when the sea
calls the hot wind home
with the question

what have you been doing

DEAR A.G.

Dear A.G., sky and sea have pulled grey blankets
over themselves. So much rain,

the earth goes on like the longest tear. Wendy
came by and called your message up to me.

She wore slippers her feet made into boats,
and as she navigated Rose Hill's minefield

of puddles sang, *Weather for ducks, girl.*
Weather for ducks for the whole hill to hear.

How I miss you – mostly for our living
and idle talk. Today, I wish you were sitting

across from me, your arms stretched over
the chair back – a *seated crucifix,* I once thought,

stunned that you wear your suffering
with such ease, the way, I suppose, we carry

our lives around, once we accept all of it.
Poems rained all day and my room is a sea

with no ground to stand on because not one,
but all betray me, and I fear I will drown:

not if you were here, listening
with your large heart for what is real in me.

ANSON ON THE OTHER END

Letters fly through cyberspace – A to J –
frequently these days. Mostly, we reduce
each other to first initials, short notes
romancing cliché, repetition: every evil
the catechism you taught warned to shun –
the hell of not saying well. Now we risk
damnation to serve a truer religion,
dispensing adjectives like medication,
shameless before typos and redundancies
that cannot say enough what we both need
in this frail season with Ken passing on,
my father's brush with death, your mother
ripening to her end. We share mere words,
unfiltered, like the speech of children.

A LETTER

If I put pen to paper
I would say
my friend
I hope life treating you right
and you walking good
now that you out there
facing the world

down here the rain
finally come bucket-a-drop
making bacchanal on zinc,
all day and night
heaven tumble down
and guess what
while I glad for the blessings
I have a bone to pick
with Mr. Nottingham
for the roof he swear
would stand up
'til the second coming
leaking
but that is a small thing
considering the earth so full
and puddles gather
all over the yard
like mini oceans,
not big like the one
you travel across

I look at them and think
how far we come
I look at them and think
that gaining never come

without a little sorrowing –
that is how things go

so I here
watching the rain,
counting my blessings
and even though the sun
not shining,
I make up songs
and cast them
like bread
on water
hoping that you too
thinking about home

ACROSS THE LINES

Across the lines our conversation tarries
again and yet again with stories we tell,
sometimes caught crossed-lined, missing
meanings we intend or lately, arriving
when the saying is spent – always a light,
soft and quivering remains in the clearing
like a day approaching its end, readied
by the hours to at last surrender itself.
So we retrace the circuits of our living,
circling the moments, spiralling to deeper
understandings. In that afterglow, I read
your celebration of Abuenameh, as I know
you too follow my father's suffering way,
and in that communion, poems flow.

ON FINDING STRENGTH

I have been waking with this on my lips:
I love you — only the other side of the bed is empty,
except for the usual litter of books, yesterday's paper,
my notebook, an endangered pair of glasses.
No body, no warmth that will roll over —
just this candid declaration, real
as the breaking day reveals all the night embraced.
Once, I decided you were a dream spilled
from another place and I had to shove you back in
before this life began its traffic in cheap faith.
Now I write your words down as often as they come,
read them back to myself, without my glasses on,
and grow strong in the response.

MOSTLY, ON EVENINGS

Mostly, on evenings, I want to write a poem
about love – full of passion and searching
tenderness, overflowing with thanksgiving,
the way I imagine your loving me will be,
if only I could reach deep enough into my dark
to find you waiting for me – as always,
expecting my homecoming. Mostly, I dream
of rivers flowing without hurry through a rain-
soaked valley, as I feel your moving through me
will be – my very being with you the one mystery
you will ever want to offer back to me,
like a strange flower found on a forest path
we walked together, without name, only scent
and colour and texture – pure wonder.

YOU SAY SUCH SIMPLE THINGS

You say simple things like *every day is*
a new flower, ok – I nod my surrender,
holding firm the anchor of your stare.
Is this how it will be? – the you in me
mothering my lost things, cracked but whole,
your faith an old innocence, the way I feel
good poems should be – time-bruised but free.
I want to write your poems; yet they come hard.
I want to bring you them, treasures I find
in the rubble of my living, like the conversation
I recorded from the road: *Which part Sunday is,*
down so? The answer: *Nah, Sunday home.*
A simple wisdom breathes in such a naming.
                              Sabbath is at home.
Close to my heart you rest,
rising and falling like my breath. I reach for you,
and end a child dancing on tiptoe, arms
outstretched, fingers fluttering, calling
after doves that flee the ground.

AS I WORKED ON

As I worked on, I thought only of you –
my love emptying her all into the hours
as they passed by like a waiting-room clock
drags the feet of time. As I worked on,
I thought only of you – my love weeping
at your tomb, each second another dying
on a day so wounded by loss every tomorrow
was a shadow as I worked on. I thought
of you – my love holding strong as she painted
her rooms in soft colours like a world
dreaming of renewal on a day when waiting
was longer than any death, the silence louder
than any sound as I worked on, holding
strong the walls of the hours from falling
down, as I painted a sun with you
completely gone – my love would not stop
asking the living for you – as I worked on.

KISS ME BEFORE I READ

Kiss me before I read — for you. Am I
the one dreaming again? Is it you?
Ask: I will give flesh, blood, new life — again.
But first, kiss these lips before I read my love,
bless my mouth to sing this truth. You see,
I confess it: no poem is singular, a word
unanchored to a heart. Not even a mirror
gives back nothing to the face that looks in.
The thing is to look in. I have been side-glancing
my life so long, I hadn't even noticed
the mirror broke and you have been sitting
right in front of me with your Anansi grin,
waiting for me to finally fall into my pond.
So kiss me. I will awaken to your salt.

"Must she always speak in ironies?
Doesn't she hear herself?"

"Oh, let the lady be. Isn't that the point anyway —
about writers I mean?"

"What? Am I missing something?"

"That they get us reading."

ANOTHER VERSION

Always something escapes the first telling –
versions spun from a way of seeing,
not distortions, just tales where a certain
innocence shivers with each saying
like a translation offers, without malice,
an understanding that builds the bridge,
makes possible the meeting, and what's more –
the returns to retrieve lost things,
having no words, then, to transport them.
So always, these multiple approaches
like a neophyte walking a labyrinth,
testing the paths, facing the dead, turning
new ways to learn, at last, the centre
slips away only to keep us going, there.

A RETURN TO QUINAM BAY

PROLOGUE

Ansong, seasons come to close in us all.
One Saturday, a day drenched by rain
enough to feel past blessing to mourning,
I journeyed with Andy to Quinam Bay,
that poet's chosen witness to his end . . .
or was it a beginning? Where *the road's
a black canal to sea*, he came burdened
as Colon did, with his share of darkness:
histories he had made and inherited.

On that ragged shore, I looked out and back
to where my own story began: a bay
bordered on the west by tattered jhandis,
testing breeze: on the east, an ancient river
strolls to sea where bathers like believers
wash in waters blessed with mercy salt.

A good sightseeing companion –
that is Andy: on time, travels light and
doesn't mind if I drive. Some collision
when he began did him in. I understand
perfectly what bad starts can do a body.
I tell him about my fear of flying
and that makes us fit for easy going.
So we are happy – cards on the table,
with me at the wheel and he talking
about court cases and frauds, budgets
and laws. I listen gratefully to his litany
of woes and say: *Interesting how
we're shaped by our jobs.* He nods
and shows his corn: *from writing reports.*

II

There are no accidents of discovery.
I go back a long time with Andy.

That frees us to change our minds, alter
scripts just to tease, like our wild detour

into Chaguanas, hunting for the monkey-
house of fiction, then finding it, sat

flattened before the bland white-
washed facade, until Andy announced

doubles like the answer to a riddle.
We left to serve that hunger, loving

more the road and the writer's book.
So when the vendor asked if the madam

wanted pepper, Andy turned on his charm:
she want it slight, and smiled back at me,

mischievously. So our game began —
going south to Roach's bay, only Andy,

a glutton for fact, is a slow convert:
Policing a lawless country not easy.

I know the story, so I wake the poet
in the back seat who fills him in

minus one small detail. (Morbidity
is bad company on a journey).

We chat on, high on elation,
as travellers write home in superlatives.

III

Put simply, it was a day of missing signs:
at the San Fernando Bypass circling back
to where we came and beginning again,
with Andy blaming a little too seriously
the *Mickey Mouse* scale of the interchange,
as if the model had usurped the real.
How to read this habit of constructing
every highway one lane at a time? Faith?

Not so the economy that lines the road
from Palmiste to Penal – an architecture
built to announce permanence restyles
an ancient India in concrete and steel.
We pronounce words aloud as we drive by,
as children sound language for meaning.

IV

Quinam Bay: a history within reach,
a loss we could recover in a day.
We suffer the slow traffic to Debe,
a town on the edge of idle cane fields,
doing swift trade in sweets of an India
once harnessed to stalks of bitter sugar.

Arriving there is to witness the miracle
of renewal from the ashes of that past.
Like tourist-pilgrims we join the crowd
gathered at stalls calling for delicacies
in a language unleashed from any caste –
free of geography, at last. So eating
is to savour the long labour of hands.

V

The truth is we pretend to be married —
Andy and me, on the road to making
history real. The act chose our company,
like fiction weds fact to court belief.
It was almost too easy like becoming
tourists at the Penal market, seeing
the known with a visitor's wonder,
the way geography can be the chemistry
that makes strange the familiar.

Andy wears his wedding ring mounted
at the back with tape. He has lost weight.
We talk of everything, except what
connects and separates us: Joseph's death,
Hazel's leaving. He still speaks in plurals
and I keep my own counsel, going . . .

Maybe language is freest in its cadences
as history is never citizen of any page,
only a shadow of what the heart houses
like bread in the half light of its chapel.
So the car eats the miles between Penal
and Siparia in slow time, with the poet
sleeping in the back oblivious to potholes
that threaten to connect the poles,
dreaming, I suppose, of the speech
in parenthesis. What if I say (Joseph died
believing he was cursed for loving
out of turn, and that he cried
when I said *foolishness* and kissed
first his hand, then his swollen head
where acres of brain already excised
had left him only half his self – the part
that cared or feared to know his end;
and as he closed his eyes asked, again,
why and left me holding his question.
If I told you I loved him, at seventeen,
when I wore white socks and neat pleats,
and his morning step was a music beat
trained to the boom-box he carried, large
as I imagined his heart must be, for me),
would that be enough for a history?

Siparia is a reservoir of faiths,
streaming once a year to La Divina
like a river reversing to its source.

From the summit of La Pastora,
she looks down to base at High Street's
busy commerce and carnival of signs.

B-MOBILE, DIGICEL and KFC turn tricks
to win converts. In that mas' of ads,
we miss our mark and find Soparee Ke Mai.

It is best to make light of error,
so confessing to lapsed churchgoing we enter:
two lukewarm sceptics sightseeing faith.

Andy swivels his ring like a rosary bead
and I think of the Lady's many identities –
in that small icon continents traffic.

VIII

I suppose in the end we prayed hard
from whatever store of faith we had saved
from the wreckage of our arrivals.
Something small – the woman's mantra
at the chapel's door, the mainland making
hazel her eyes, the colour of Andy's loss,
but an old east changed to another race
at that southern gate of all beginnings.

Something is always salvaged –. We gave
what we could – an offering much too small
to lift the great stone that weighed on her;
but if prayer labours to save what is precious,
then in that church where Divina levitates
like a ladder between worlds, we prayed.

Every thing lost will come back to us —
in the end — changed by the pathways
it travels to find us again, as love
will never leave us orphans in any
geography or history. We are fully
ourselves, here, and much more
of what we have not yet dreamed,
even when vestiges, worn but dear
as memory, are all the possessions
we carry and, being all, they blossom
larger than death itself as Roach
discovered when a lily seeded in rock
opened, unburdened of the sorrows
his verse laboured with less belief
to set free in a metre beyond grief.

X

A narrow passage to bay is Quinam.
Migrant hardwoods far from their origins

roof us with generous leaves that bleed.
"Look," Andy called from the bank,

showing me to belief – crimson palms upheld.
The light dimmed further then,

and we stood a second too long,
held, in that sudden return to the dead.

On this coast, a history began with a lost
discoverer who drew whole continents

into his narrative: Andy's India
my mixed and uncertain heritage, planted

like those trees in earth not alien to itself –
native, as we who travel to an arrival.

After tunnelling through teak,
an entry into light, stark,
despite a heavy sky.

Glare slaps us alive.
We pause, stunned blind
by the horizon leaping

mercilessly into sight
before vanishing past
any seeing. Slowly,

the asphalt road
reappears like a mooring
and we veer left,

crunching to shore
on the tide of a declaration
or question: *We reach*

Does every arrival begin
with that split?
Not an either/

or dilemma, not difference,
but a troublesome
conjunction

that welcomes the road's end
and mourns the lost dream.

Quinam is the crib
of that remaking.

XII

I leave quite Marabella for this? —
from an Indian man standing beside me.
A question registered as a complaint,
on a beach whose name evokes a query,

its root making a demand on identity.
He was disappointed with his discovery,
as perhaps Columbus had been, his hope
of riches and glory drowned in a filthy sea;

as cargoes of Africans must have been,
arriving where they had no desire to be,
not knowing where they were exactly.
There are no guarantees; only signs to read.

We came from Tacarigua, was all I
could say. He glanced at Andy and at me.
I thought that truth might console him:
we had all suffered to meet this same sea.

XIII

The Orinoco opens its broad fan
of tributaries to the Atlantic.

Between Iere and mainland, the delta
is a bowl of diluted gold,

paving the channel Columbus' ships
first rode like a street

to the continent he sought, but missed,
thinking it a mere island.

So finding was illusion – the pastiche
of discovery like *La Concepcion*

was a cloud – the romance of encounter
made real like El Dorado's stories.

Is it always that myth makes history:
hounding a rumour to its source,

believing fiction harder than fact?
Is that the saving cross/current

of every narrative: an Anansi story
or a journey through the serpent's mouth?

XIV

To swim at Quinam is to enter a womb.
Where river-water and ocean-salt mingle
liquid warmth soothes the body like balm.

Going under, we lose sky and ground,
nothing but an aquatic cloud, a vault
empty of everything but formless sound.

We surface, grateful for that surrender
and wade to shore trailing nostalgia,
quivering like newborns greet the air.

On the shore, a girl with sargasso hair
builds a dome with greyish sand
much too close to the shuttling surf.

Wet-shone she huddles there
like some amphibian bordering worlds.
Her labour is the miracle she births.

XV

Leaving is always a return
to what escapes us coming in.

Imitation ajoupas punctuate
the muddy banks of a sluggish river.

Under leafy umbrellas barebacked men
congregate around rum bottles

and plastic coolers deliberating cards
like postmodern tribal leaders.

It is like viewing a muted nostalgia film
of a world on the threshold of loss.

Quinam now trades in ecotourism.
Signs crucified to trees prohibit:

littering, hunting, logging – everything.
They are directives mainly for natives,

set as for children in need of discipline.
Andy is pleased. The Law is his thing.

The poet sighs and sings too loudly:
Emancipate yourself from mental slavery.

I drive to keep the peace, thinking Marley
had it right: that History sail already.

Truth is in the going on. We push west
of Quinam, exceeding Mendes,
going past Roach's death sea,
following the sun to a brighter setting,
stopping at Los Bajos for drinks:
STAG for Andy,
orange juice for me,
and the poet calls for Heineken,
suddenly feeling foreign.

A wind stirs,
so we hit the road looking
for the turn-off to Los Iros,
wanting to see the name
made to mean impossible to reach.
But with the poet playing blind
and Andy studying houses,
we end instead at Erin Beach.

The road to shore divides
a group of villagers
from a preacher
armed with microphone
and music band.
Empty market stalls
backdrop the service –
a chain-linked fence
cast between them
and their small school
of not too distant souls.

St. Francis stands like a monument
on the hill – closed and quite
like a dying age.

Further in, fishermen wearing
the beach on their feet
sell fish fresh from the sea.
We buy that peace.

EPILOGUE

Stories tell no lies. Truth is always need.
So Columbus writes his sovereigns tales
of New World Valencia greens, selling

his discoveries to keep him on the seas.
That was his scheme and the outcome:
his journal crossed into fantasy.

Quinam is a bay west of the first lies
of discovery. Three hills that never were,
people never seen. There a poet swam

to sea to reverse history. My version:
invention was his one hope all along,
but its light dulled to night in him.

I write now to make all our stories go on.

POSTSCRIPT

ONE DAY SOMEONE ASKED

One day someone asked your name,
wanting to know the one I sang for.
Love, I tried to say, but lost my tongue.
No word, no grammar could speak
your being ever present in my blood.
Do I not know you my forever song?
Are you a fiction my need created?
If so, I'm content to write stories of you
until you become the epic of my country
and the language that makes you real.

IT BEGAN THE DAY

It began the day I sat counting coins
while my life went in search of me.
I looked up and your smile opened
with no trace of shadow as a high sun.
Blinded by your beauty, I reached out
as new fronds eager for light stretch
thin their dream to companion the sky.
But somewhere between my knowing
and my reaching you became a night
into which I stumbled so completely,
I have lost you and myself equally.
Since then, Love, I'm wary of light.

AGAIN

if they ask
I will say
simply
you are all my loves
rolled tight
like a single wave
rushing to my shore.
I advance
and
run from you
at once.

ABOUT THE AUTHOR

Jennifer Rahim is Trinidadian. Her first collection of poems, *Mothers Are Not the Only Linguists* was published in 1992, followed by *Between the Fence and the Forest* (Peepal Tree, 2002). She also writes short fiction and criticism. She currently teaches at The Liberal Arts Department, The University of the West Indies, St. Augustine, Trinidad.

Her poems have appeared in several Caribbean and international journals and anthologies. Some of these include *The Caribbean Writer*, *Small Axe*, *The Trinidad and Tobago Review*, *The Graham House Review*, *Mangrove*, *The Malahat Review*, *Crossing Water*, *Creation Fire*, *The Sisters of Caliban*, *Crab Orchard Review* and *Atlanta Review*. Short stories have appeared in *The New Voices*, *The Caribbean Writer, Caribbean Voices I* and *Anthurium*.

Awards include The Gulf Insurance Writers Scholarship (1996) to attend the Caribbean Writers Summer Institute, Univ. of Miami; The New Voices Award of Merit (1993) for outstanding contributions to The New Voices journal; The Writers Union of Trinidad and Tobago Writer of the Year Award (1992) for the publication, *Mothers Are Not The Only Linguists*.

ALSO BY JENNIFER RAHIM

Between the Fence and the Forest
ISBN: 9781900715270
Pages: 88
Published: September 2002
Price: £7.99

Like the mythical douen from the Trinidadian forests whose head and feet face in different directions, Jennifer Rahim's poems explore states of uncertainty which are both sources of unease and of creative possibility. Her forest is 'where tallness is not the neighbour's fences/ and bigness is not the swollen houses/ that swallow us all...' But it is also the place where the bushplanter 'seeing me grow branches/ draws out his cutting steel and slashes my feet/ since girls can never become trees.'

She writes of a Trinidad finely balanced between the forces of rapid urbanisation and the constantly encroaching green chaos of tropical bush, whose turbulence regularly threatens a fragile social order, and whose people, as the descendants of slaves and indentured labourers, are acutely resistant to any threat to clip their wings and fence them in.

She tells stories, her own and other people's, which dramatise the contrary desires for a neat security and for an unfettered freedom with homour, emeotional engagement and intellectual acuteness.

Songster and Other Stories
ISBN: 9781845230487
Pages: 145
Published: August 2007
Price: £8.99

Rahim's stories move between the present and the past to make sense of the tensions between image and reality in contemporary Trinidad. The contemporary stories show the traditional, communal world in retreat before the forces of local and global capitalism. A popular local fisherman is gunned down when he challenges the closure of the beach for a private club catering to white visitors and the new elite; the internet becomes a rare safe place for an AIDS sufferer to articulate her pain; cocaine has become the scourge even of the rural communities. But the stories set thirty years earlier in the narrating 'I's' childhood reveal that the 'old-time' Trinidad was already breaking up. The old pieties about nature symbolised by belief in the presence of the folk-figure of 'Papa Bois' are powerless to prevent the ruthless plunder of the forests; communal stability has already been uprooted by the pulls towards emigration, and any sense that Trinidad was ever edenic is undermined by images of the destructive power of alcohol and the casual presence of paedophilic sexual abuse.

Rahim's Trinidad, is though, as her final story makes clear, the creation of a writer who has chosen to stay, and she is highly conscious that her perspective is very different from those who have taken home away in a suitcase, or who visit once a year. Her Trinidad is 'not a world in my head like a fantasy', but the island that 'lives and moves in the bloodstream'. Her reflection on the nature of small island life is as fierce and perceptive as Jamaica Kincaid's *A Small Place*, but comes from and arrives at a quite opposite place. What Rahim finds in her island is a certain existential insouciance and the capacity of its people, whatever their material circumstance, to commit to life in the knowledge of its bitter-sweetness.

All titles available to buy online from <u>peepaltreepress.com</u>